Beach Babes

Hot Sexy Swimsuit Girls Models Pictures

By **PHOTO ART LOVER**

Copyright © Beach Babes

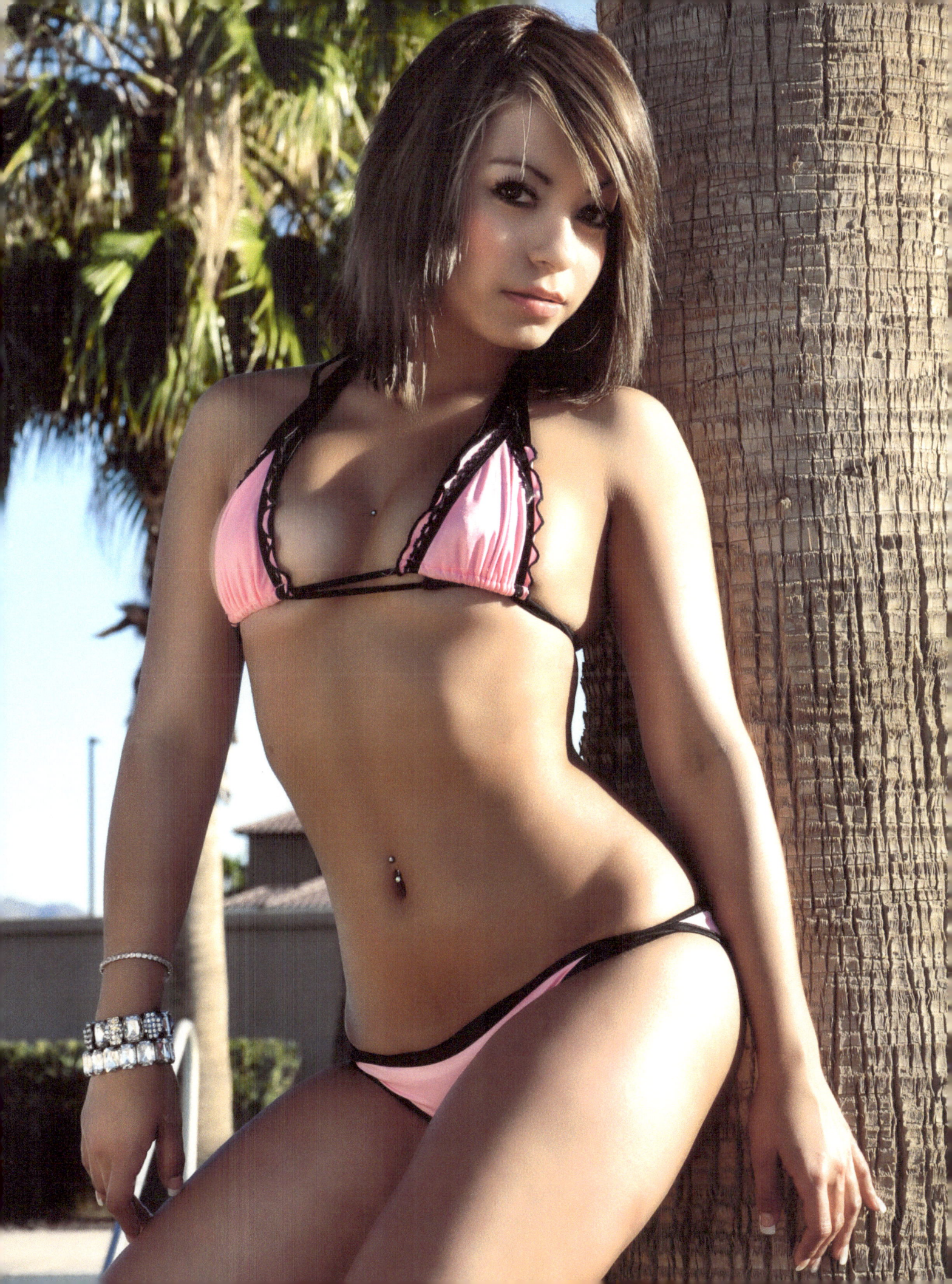

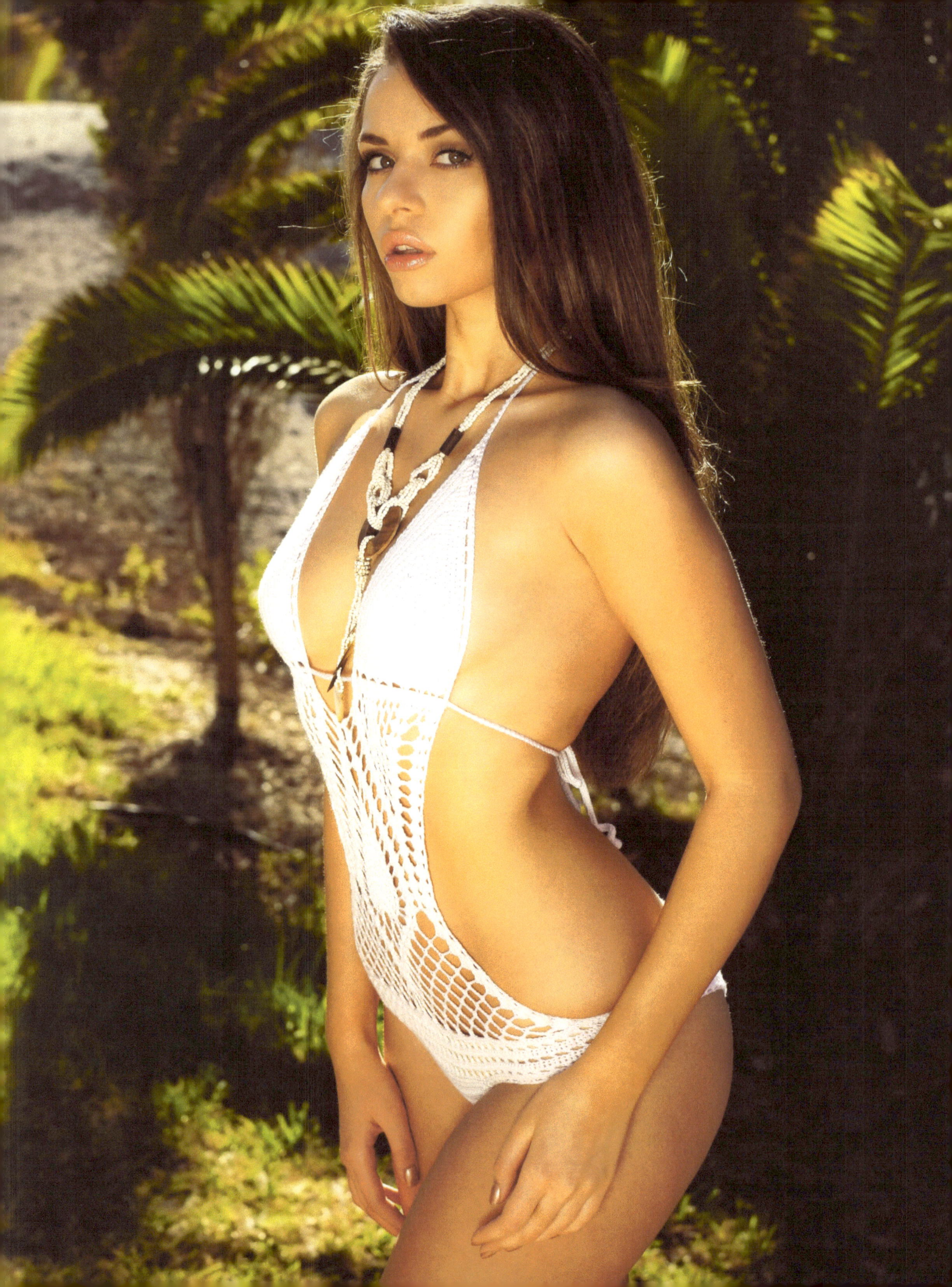

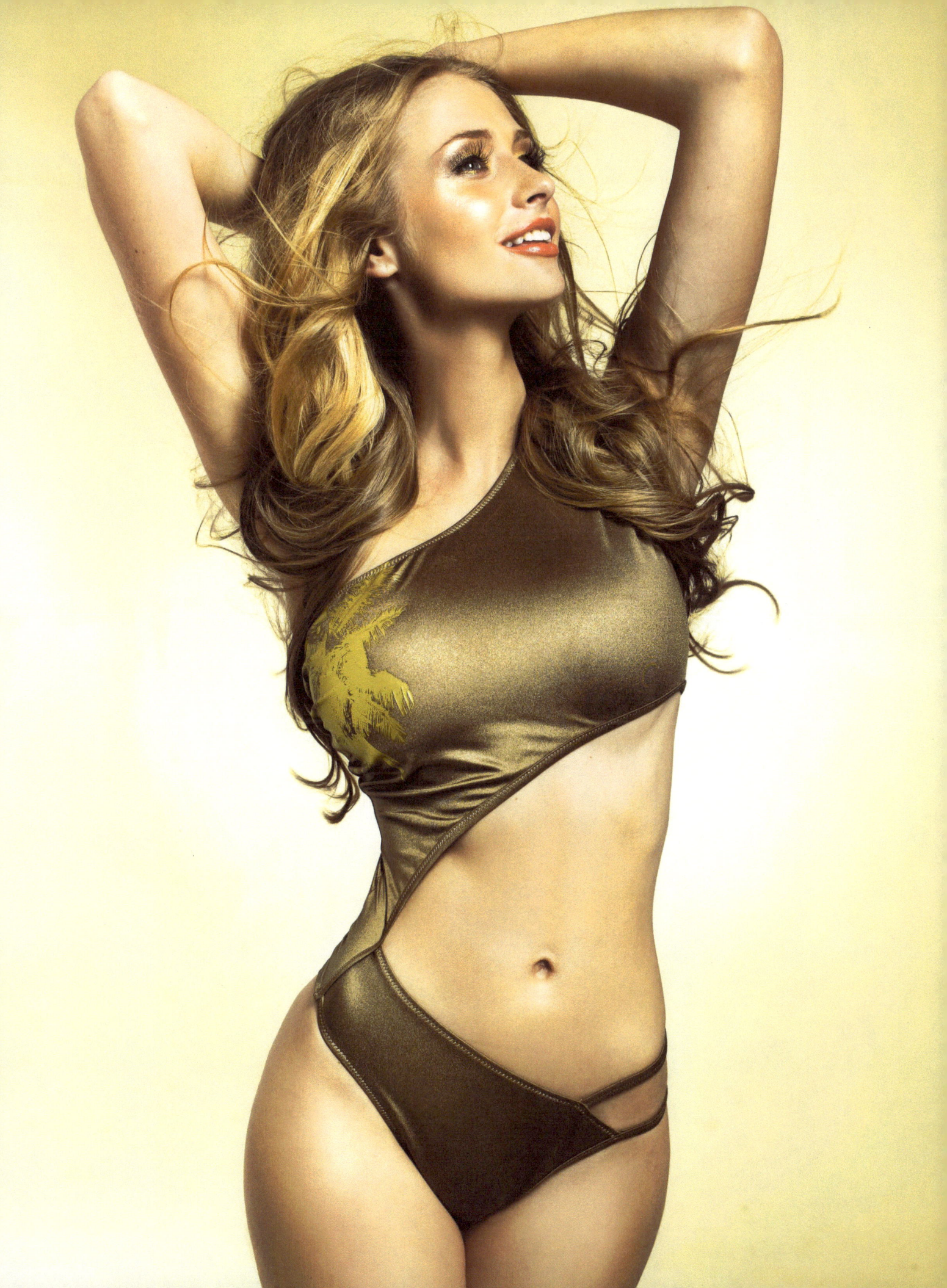

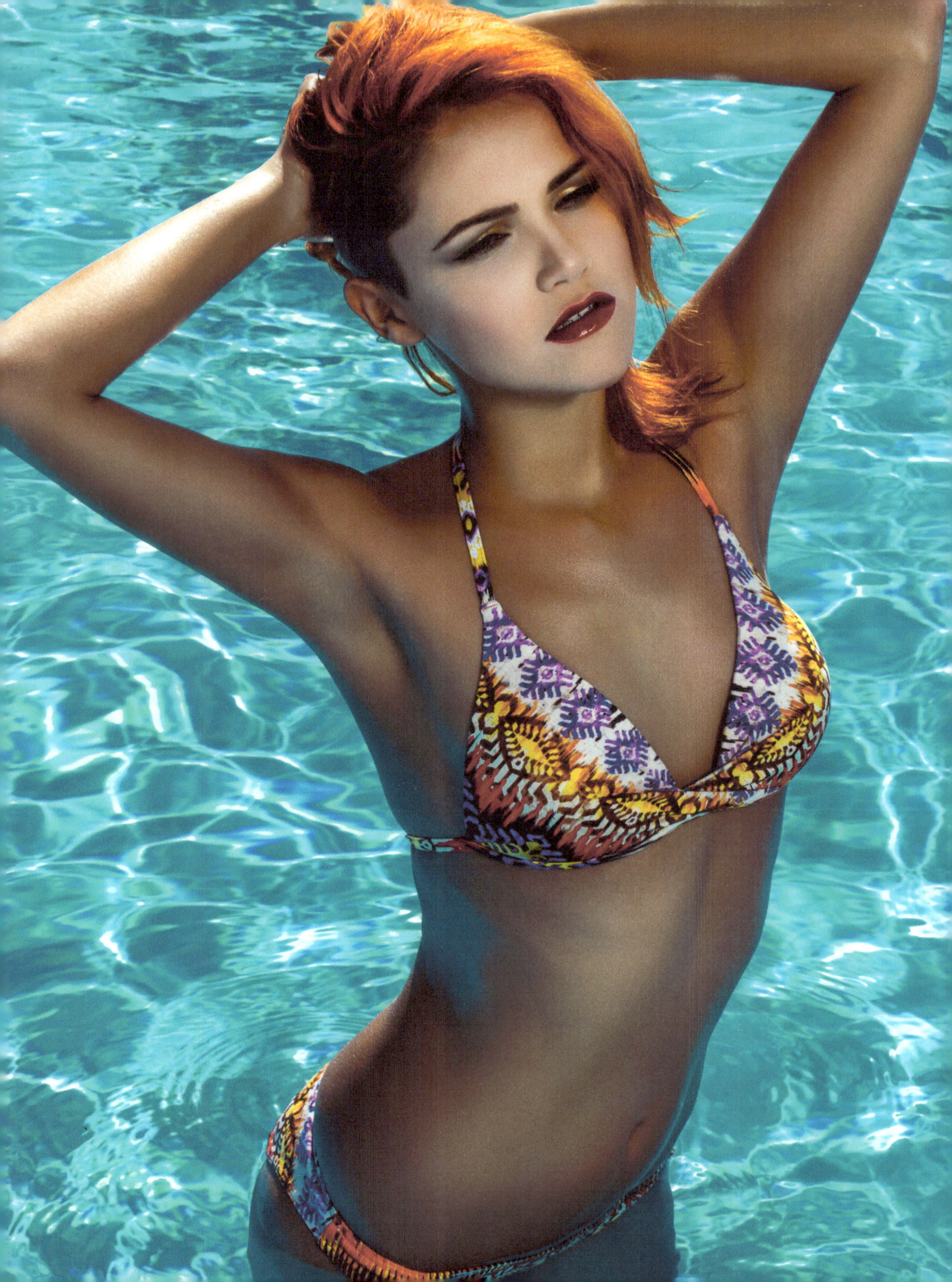

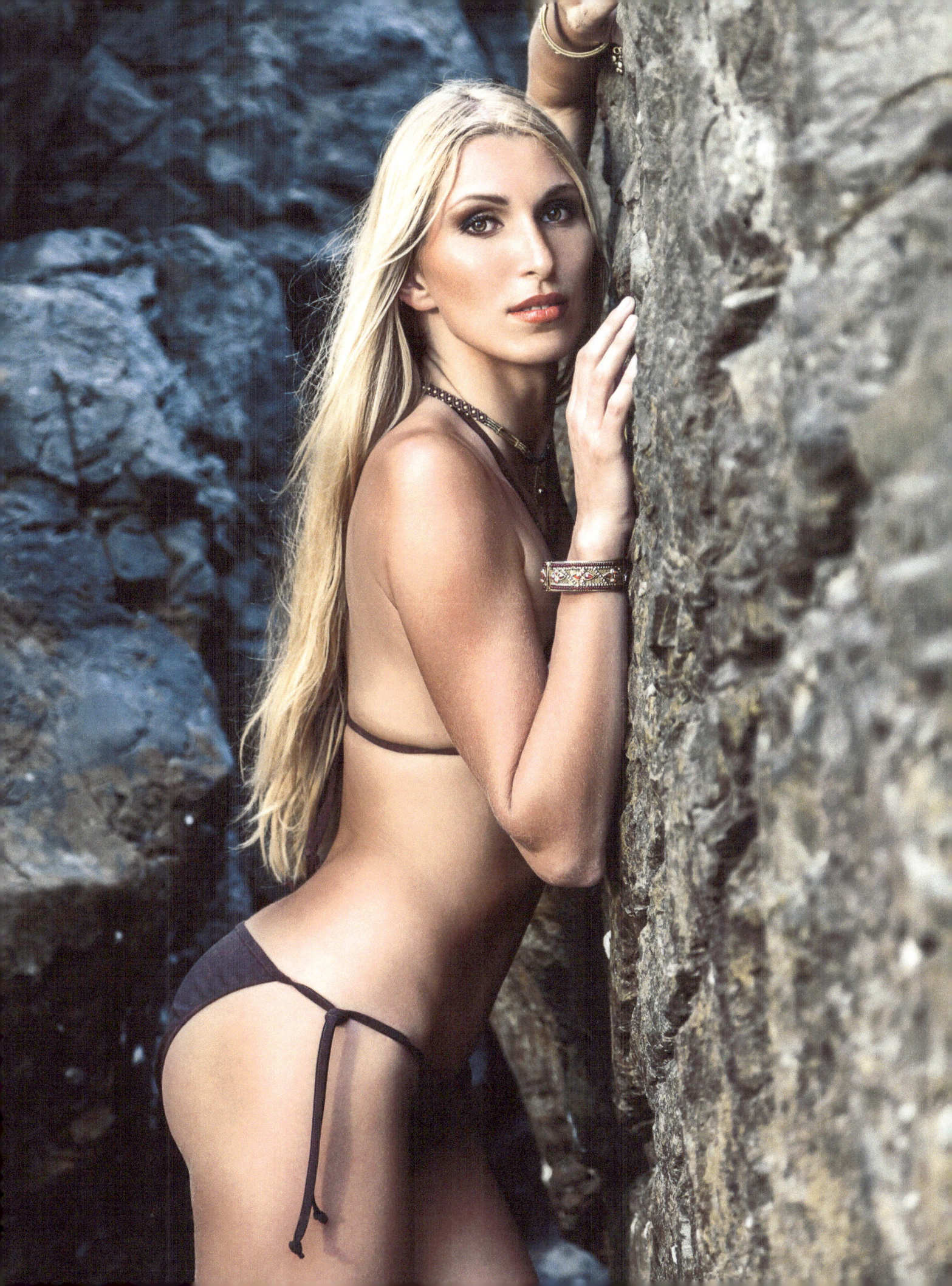

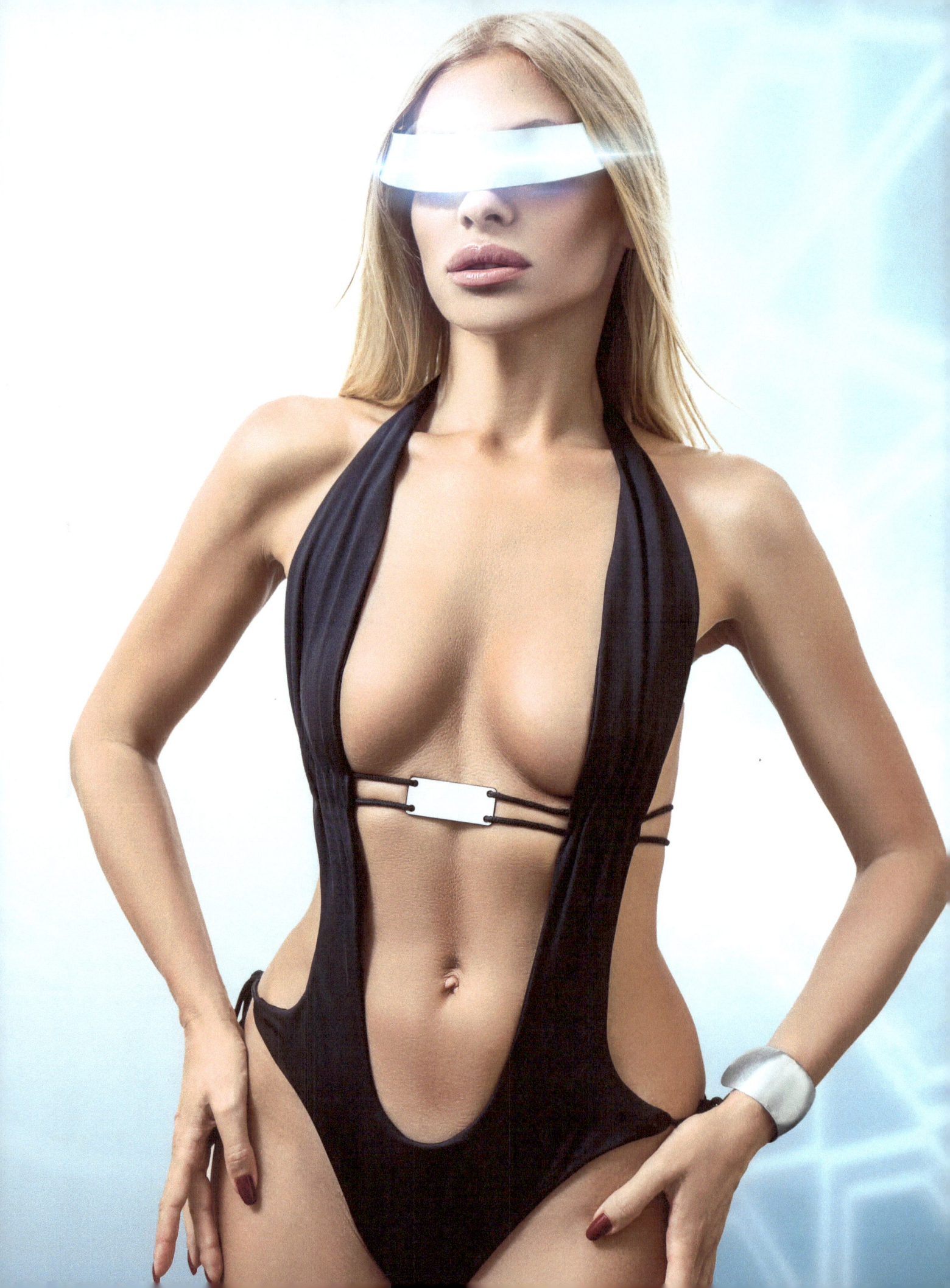

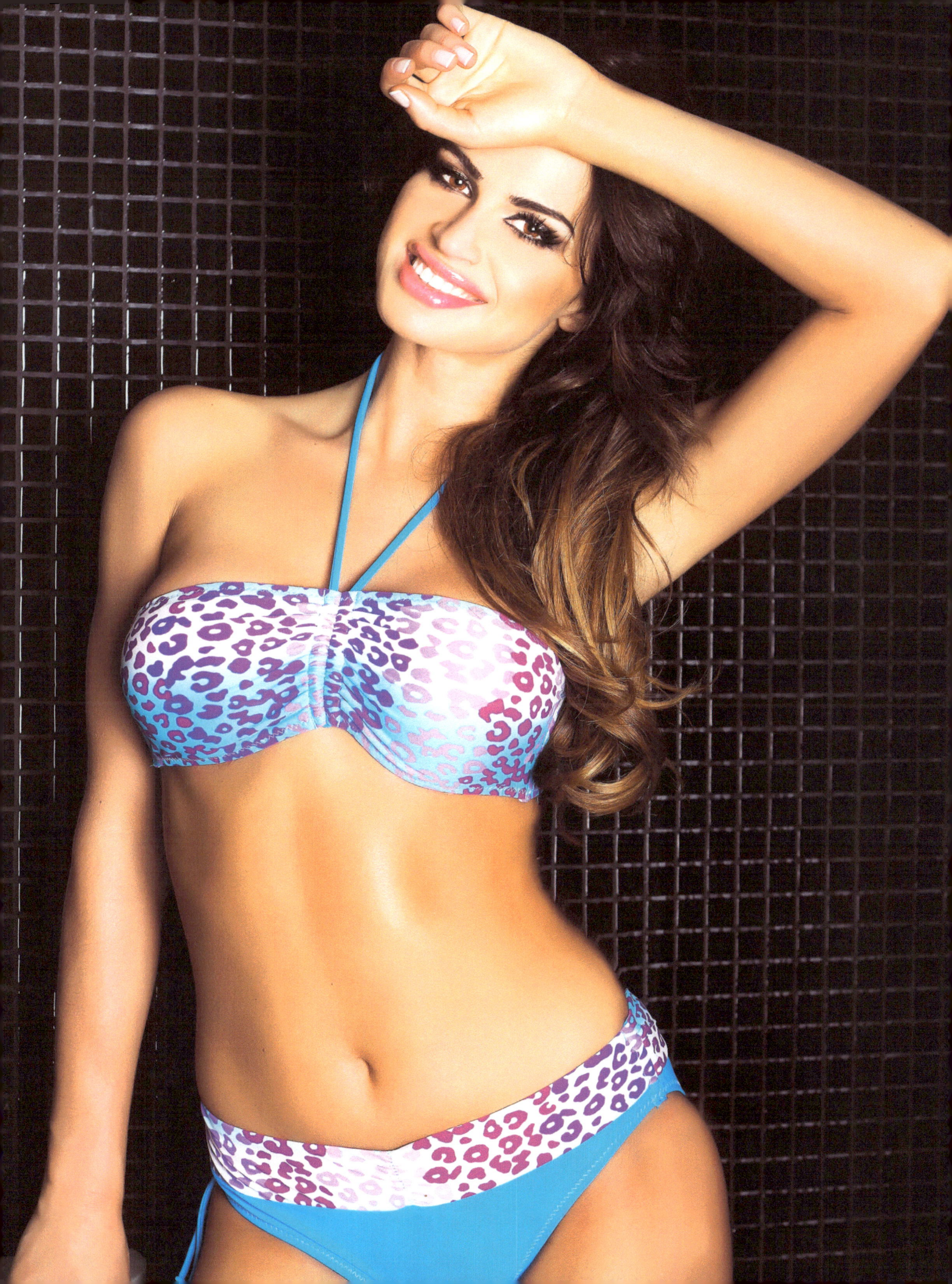

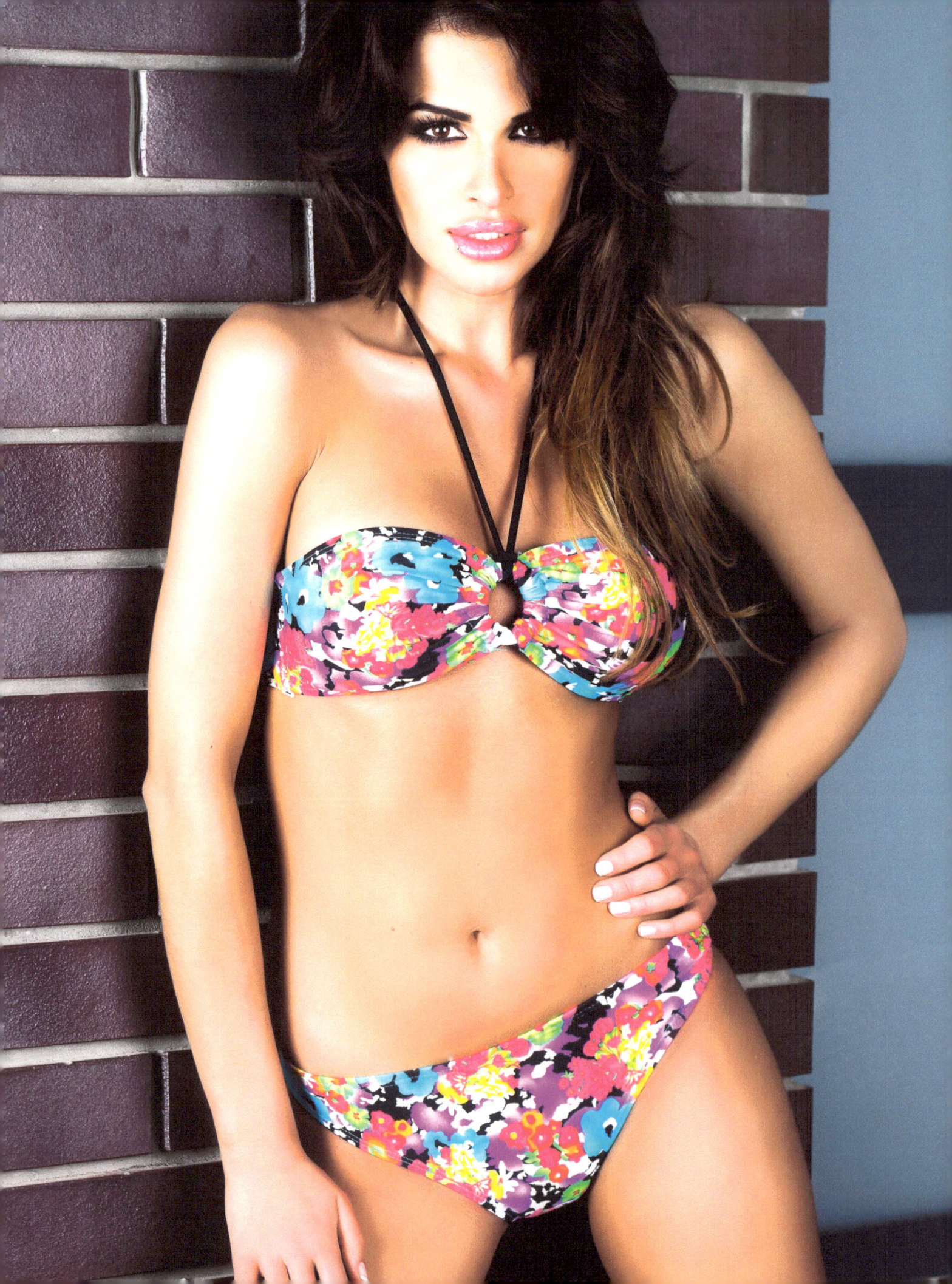

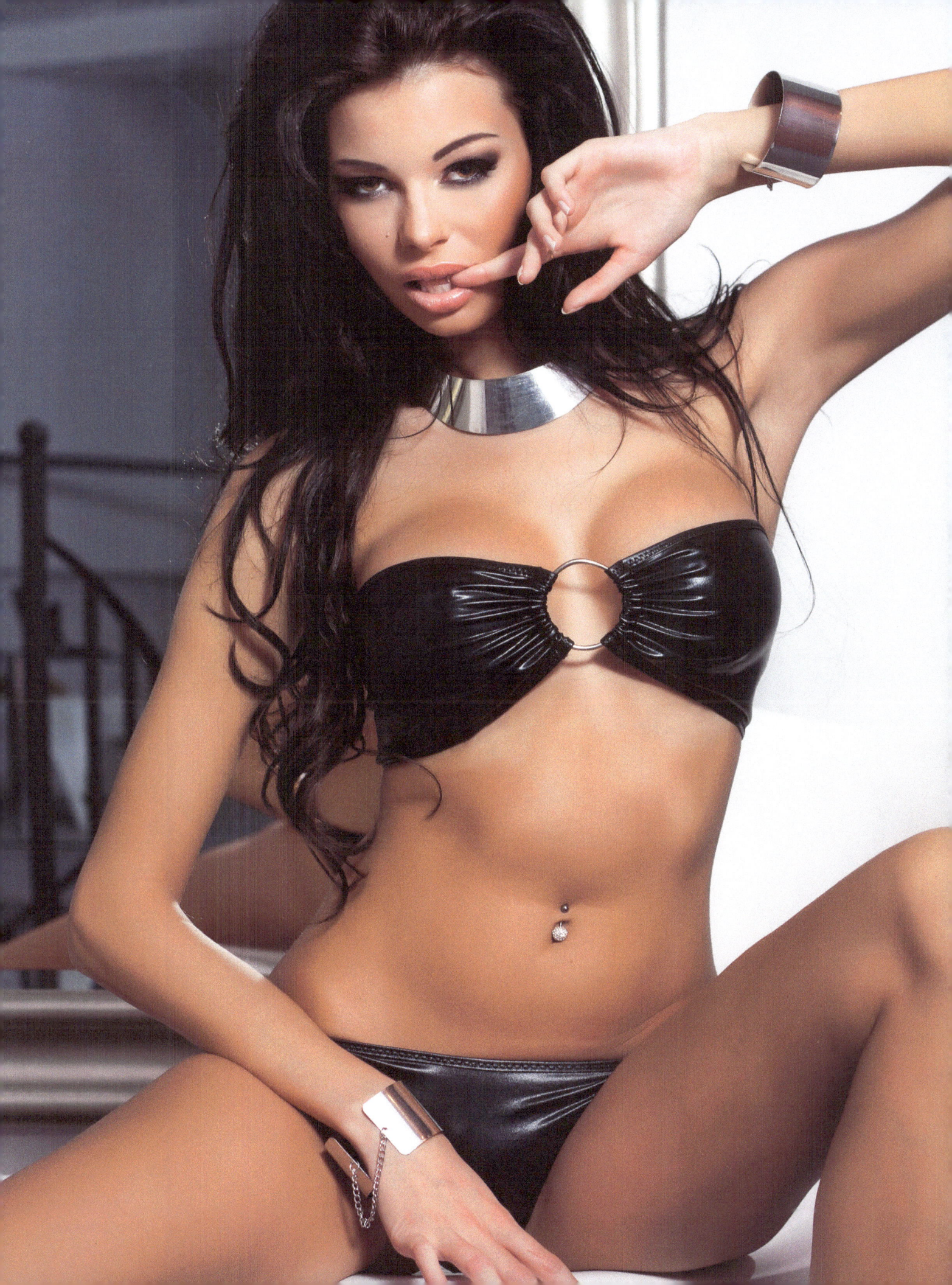

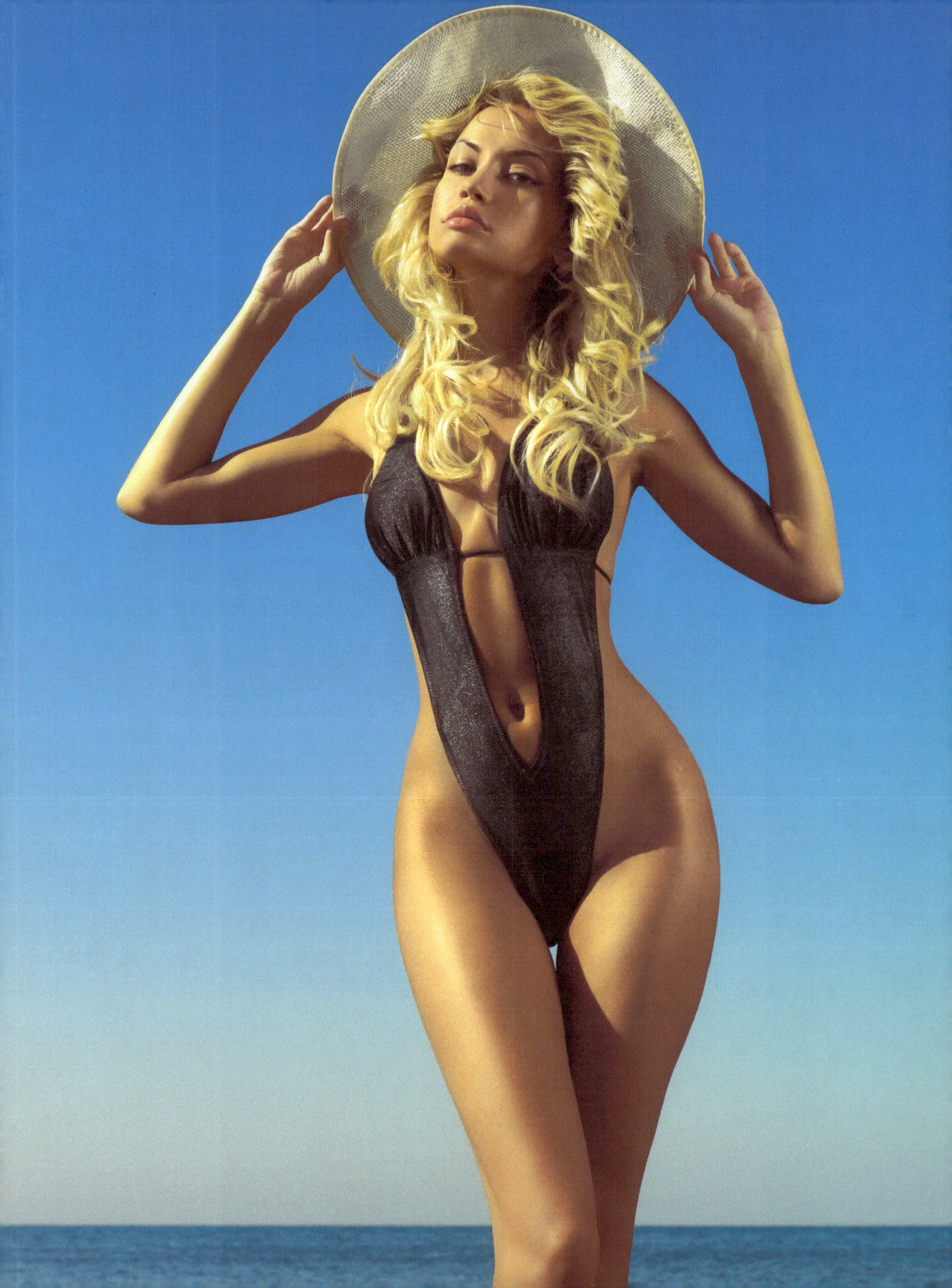

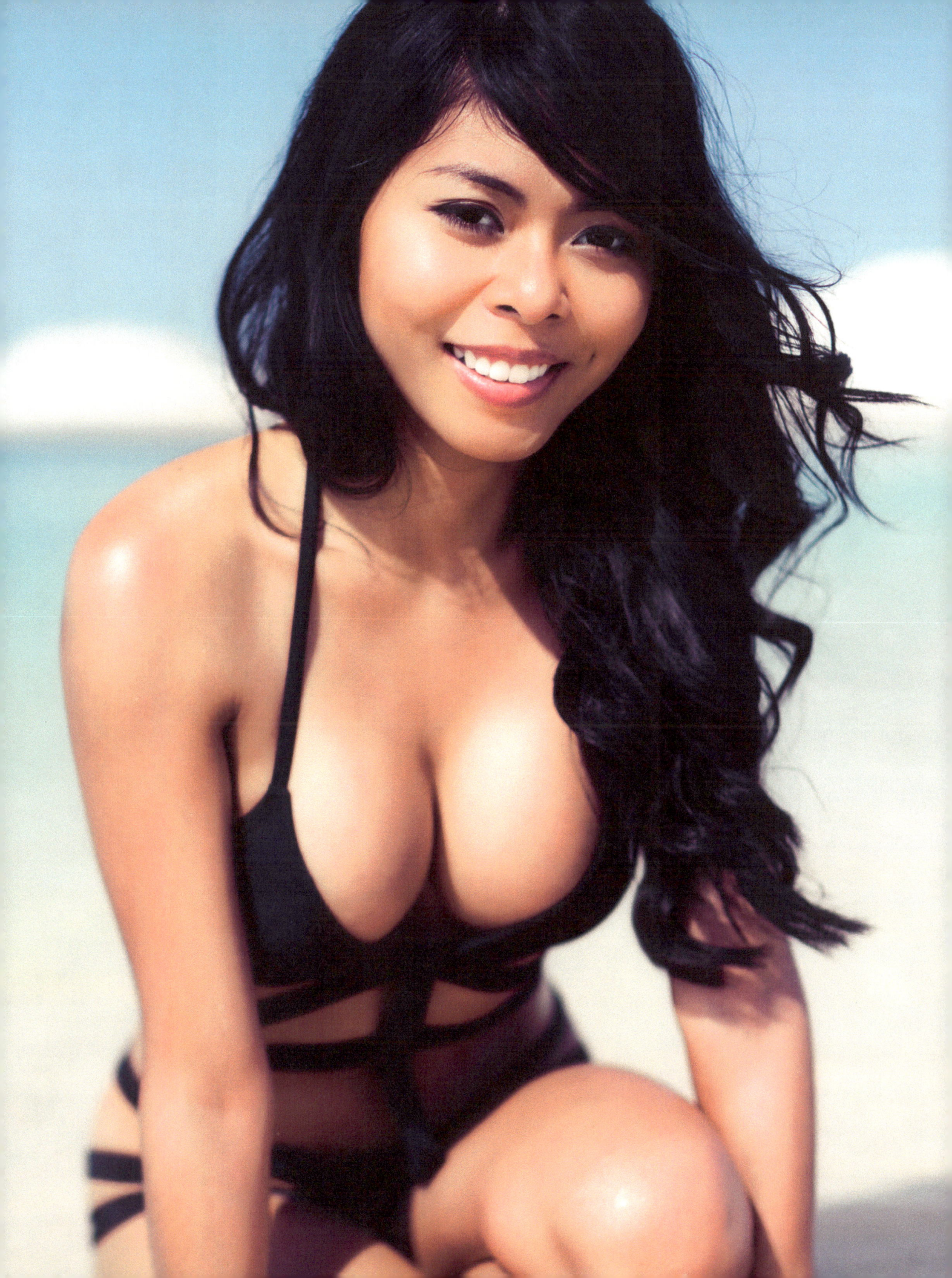

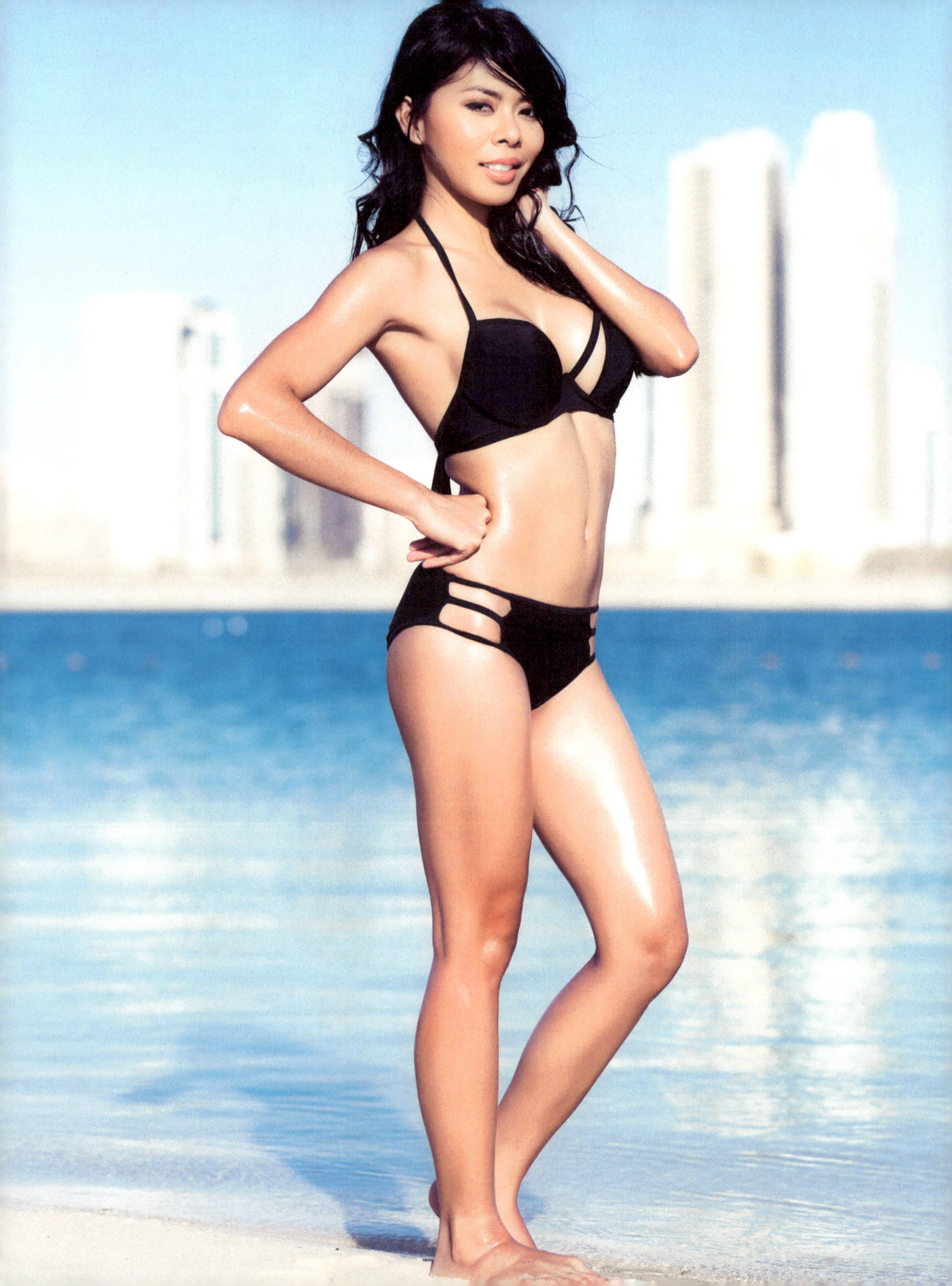

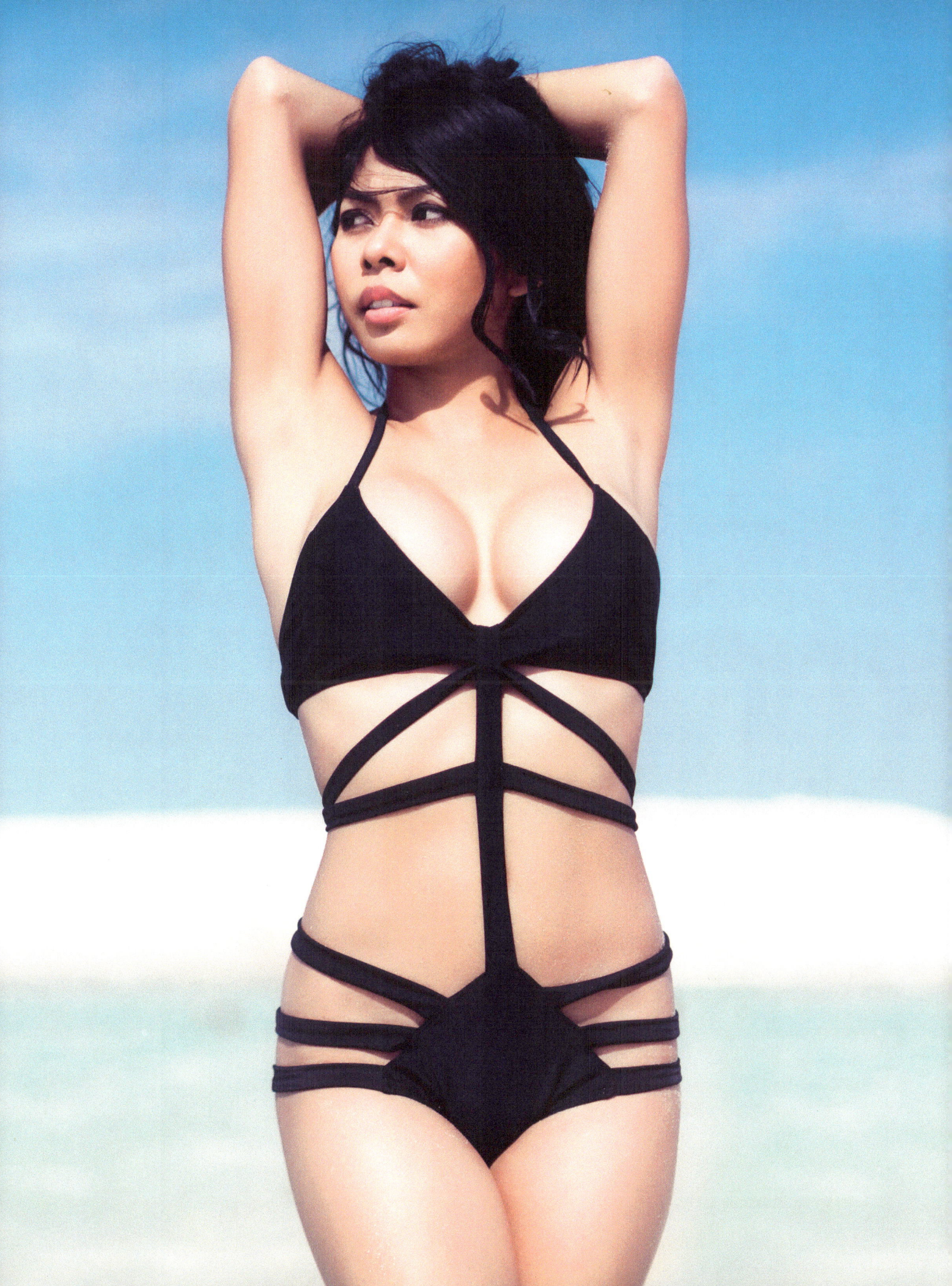

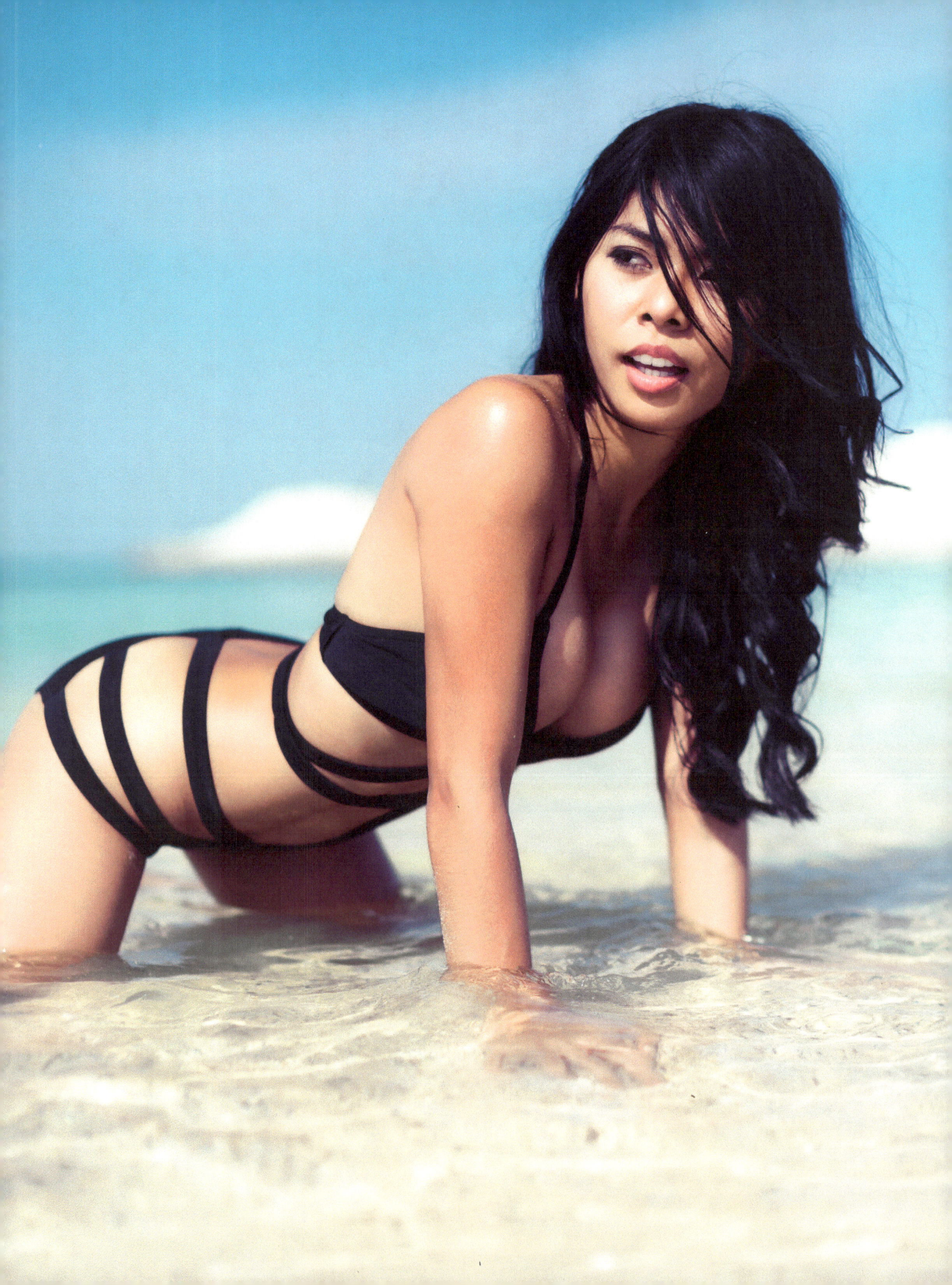

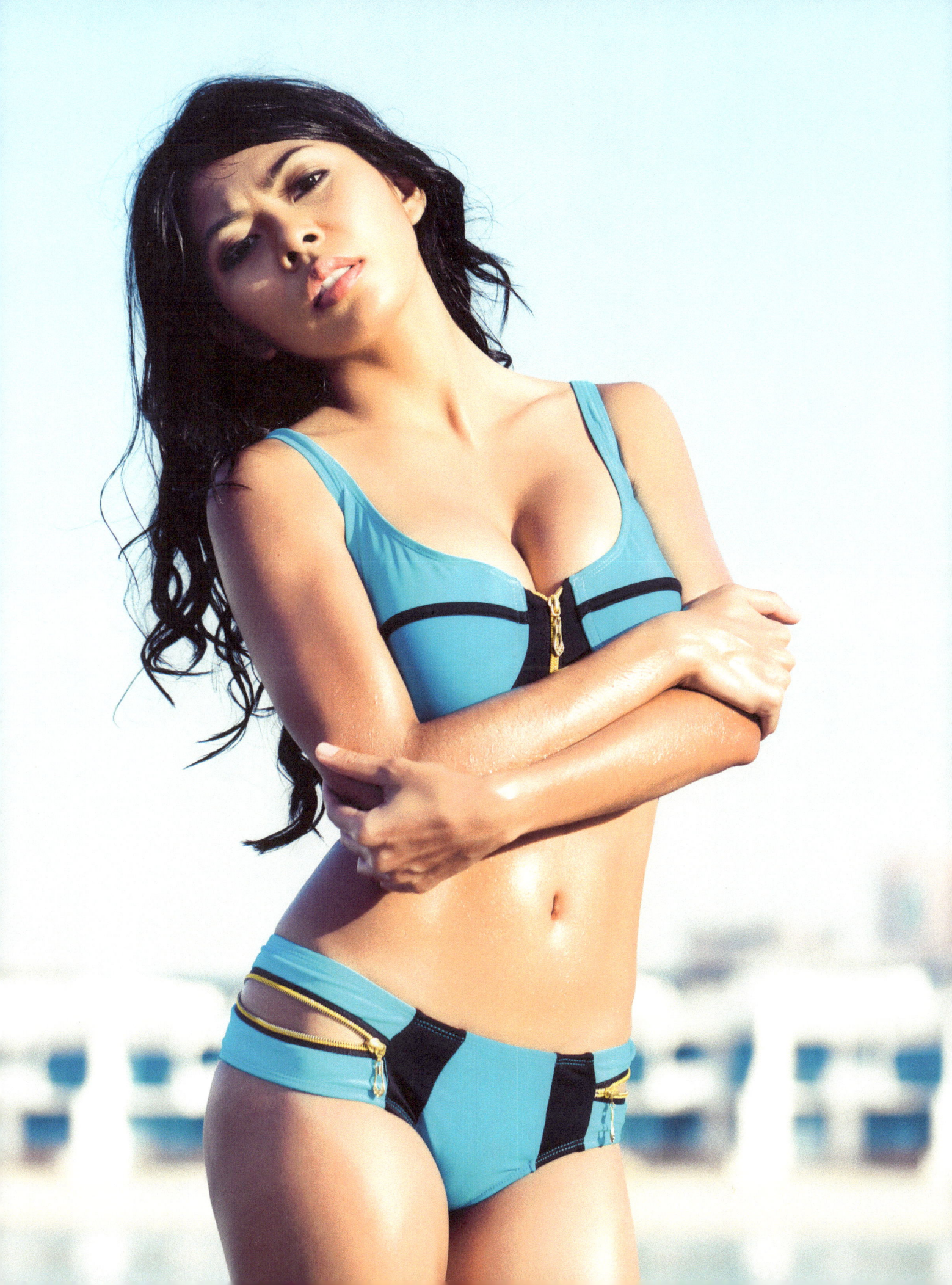

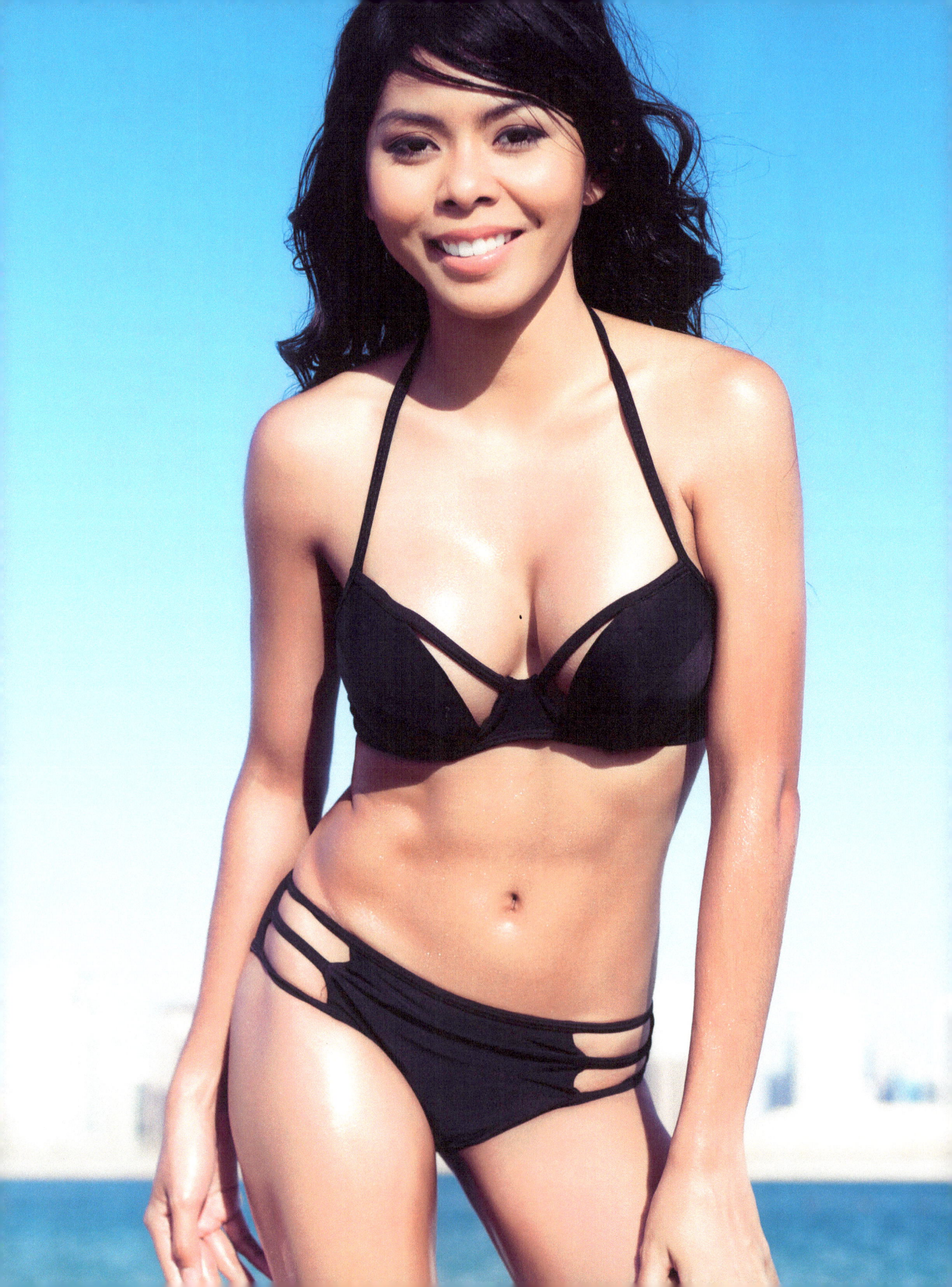

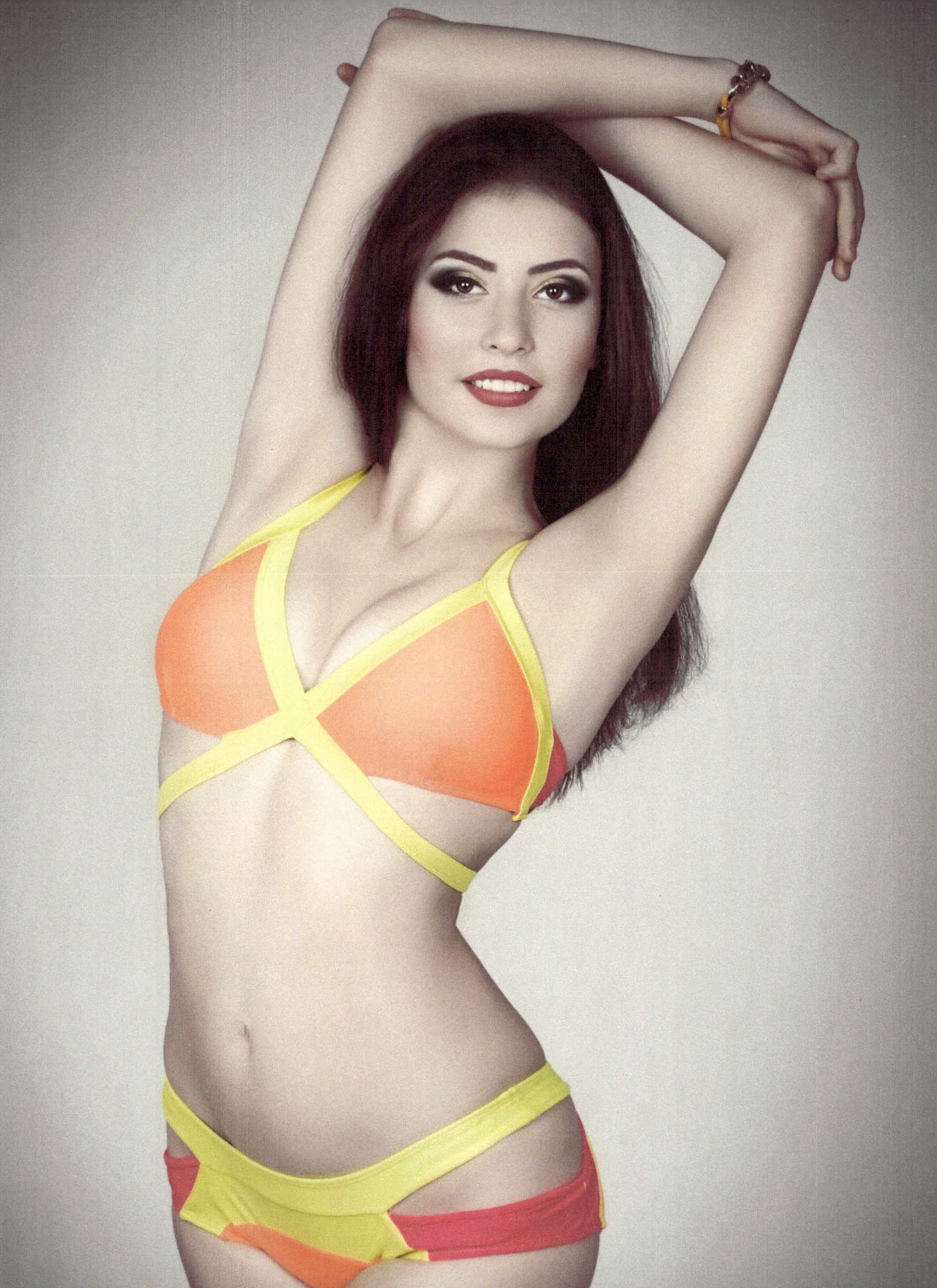

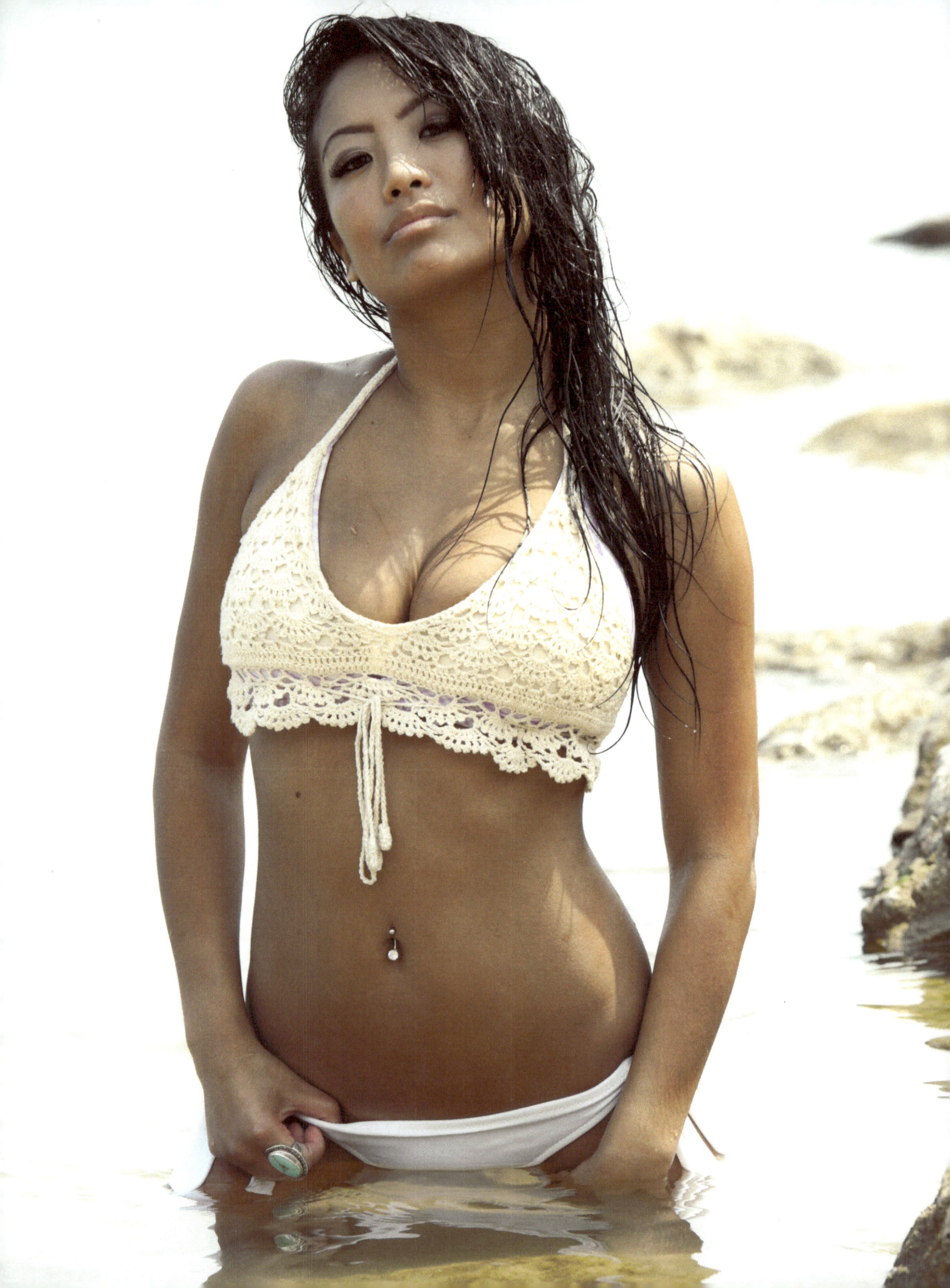

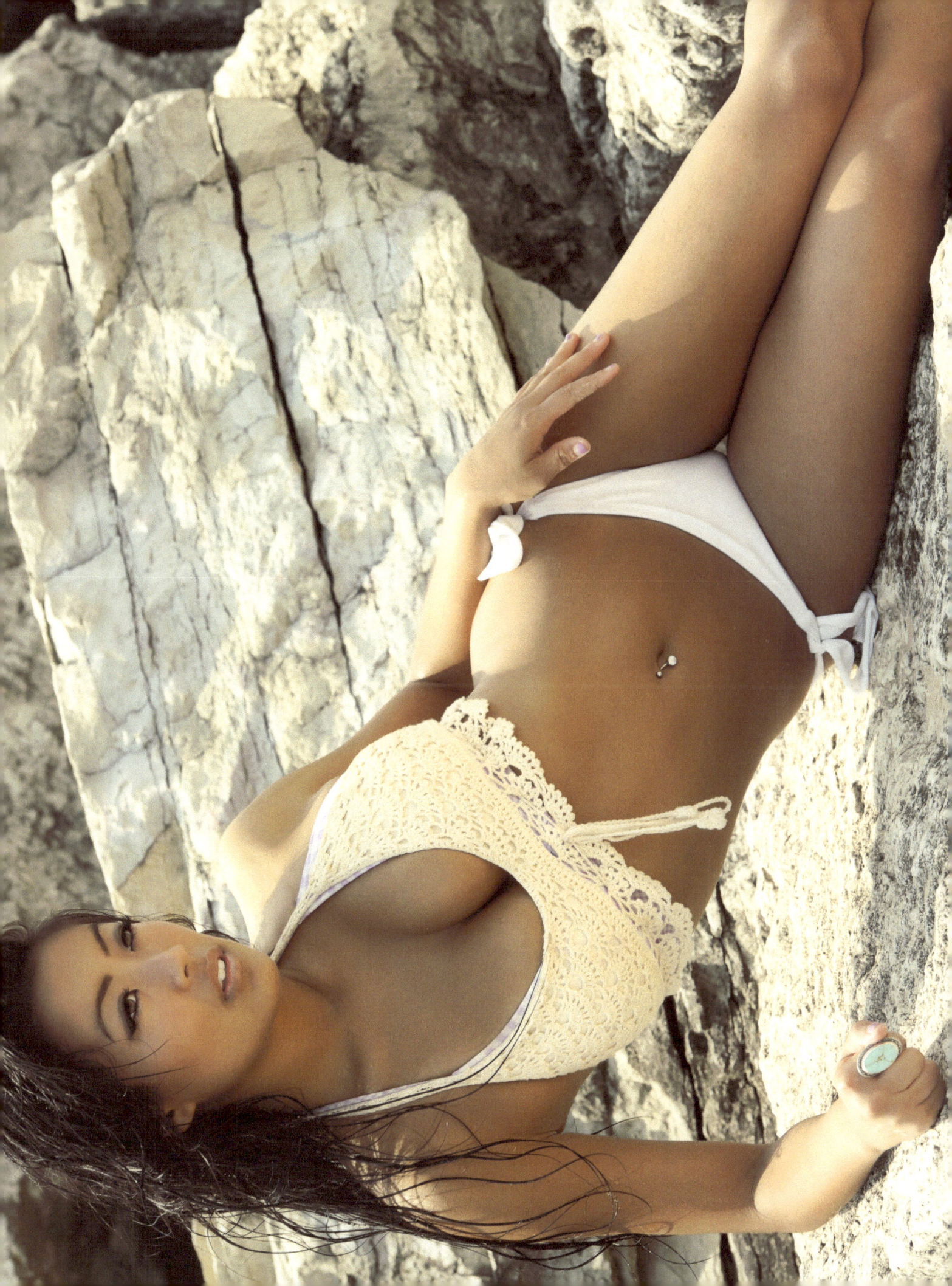

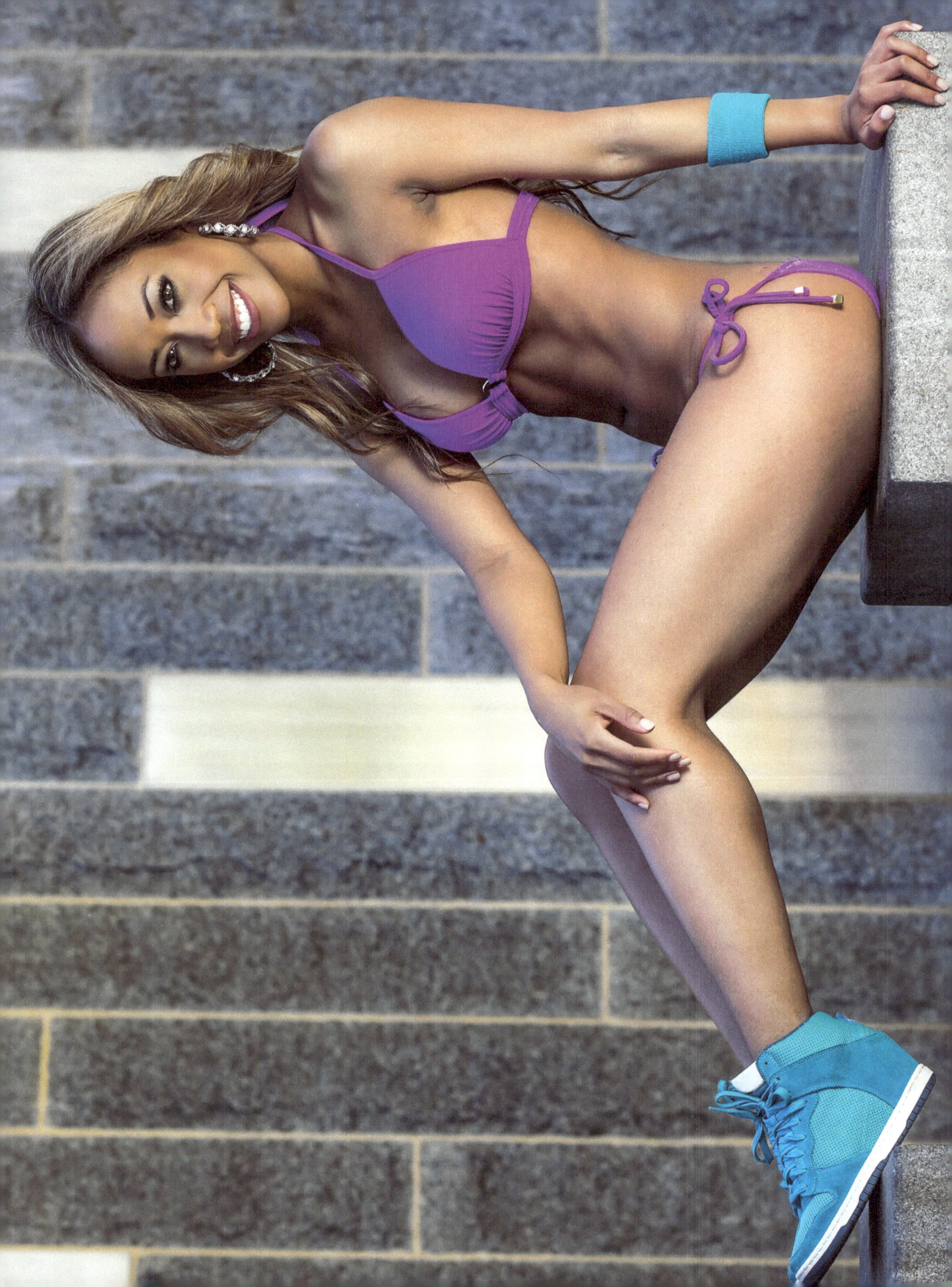

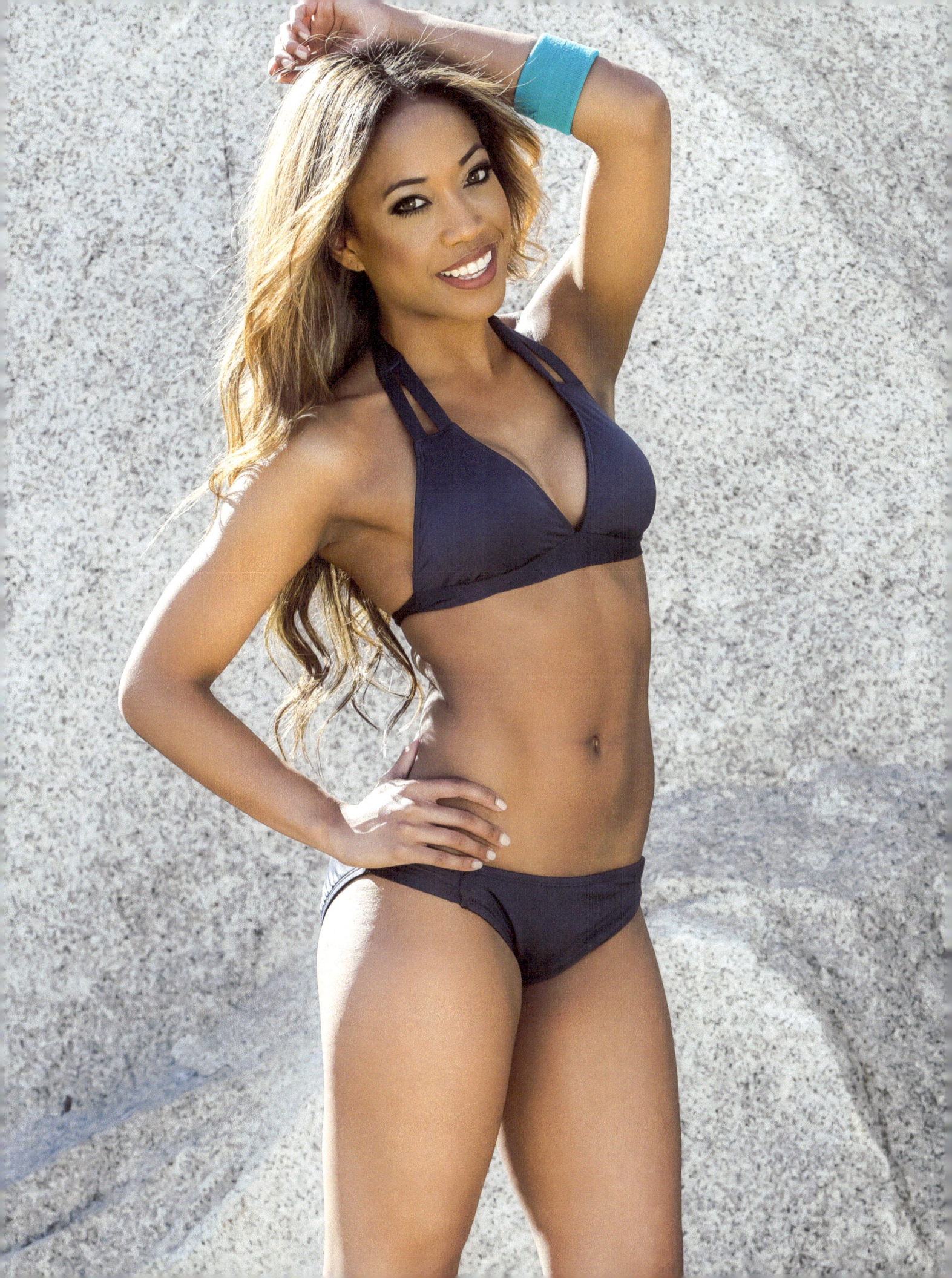

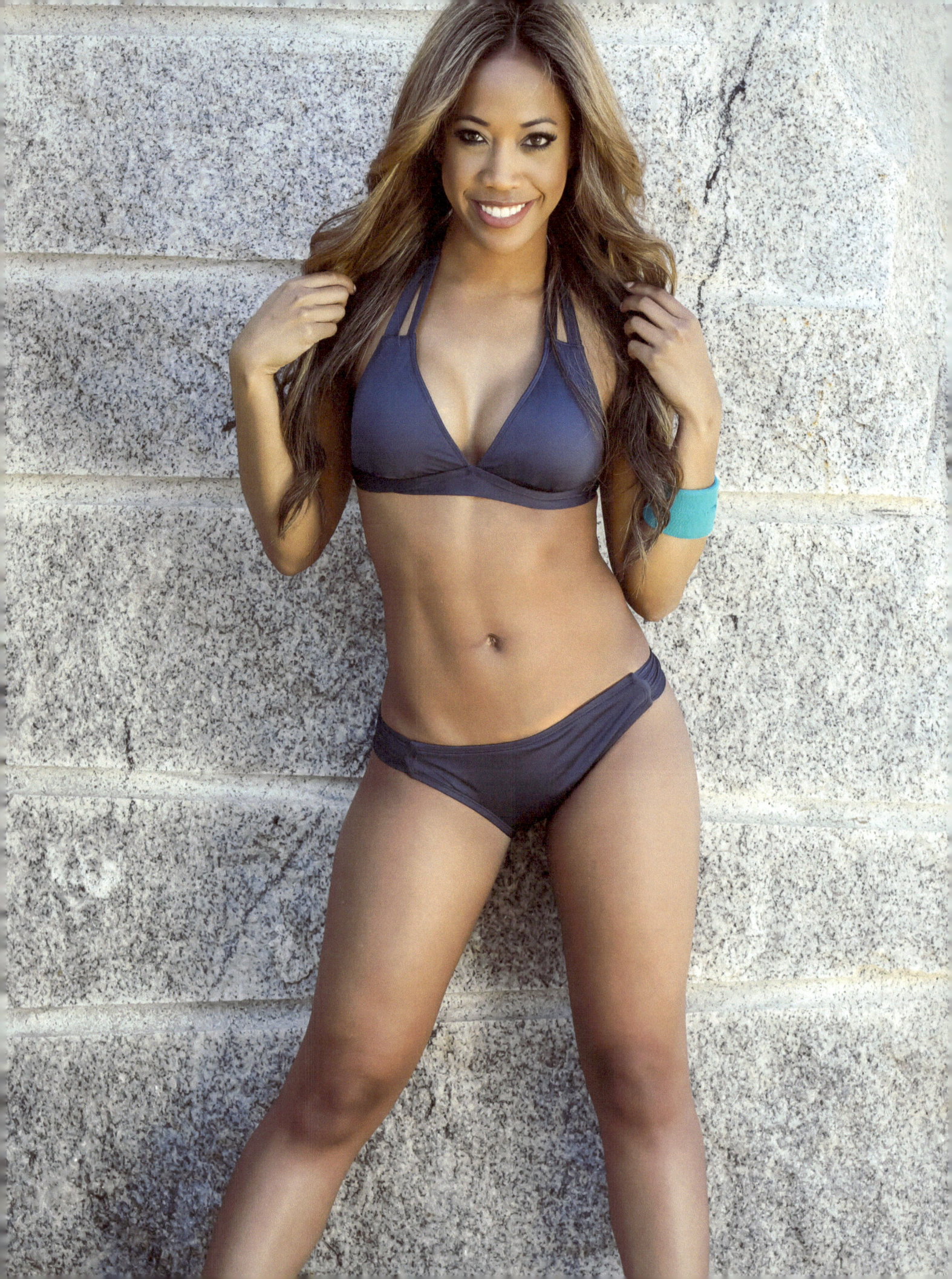

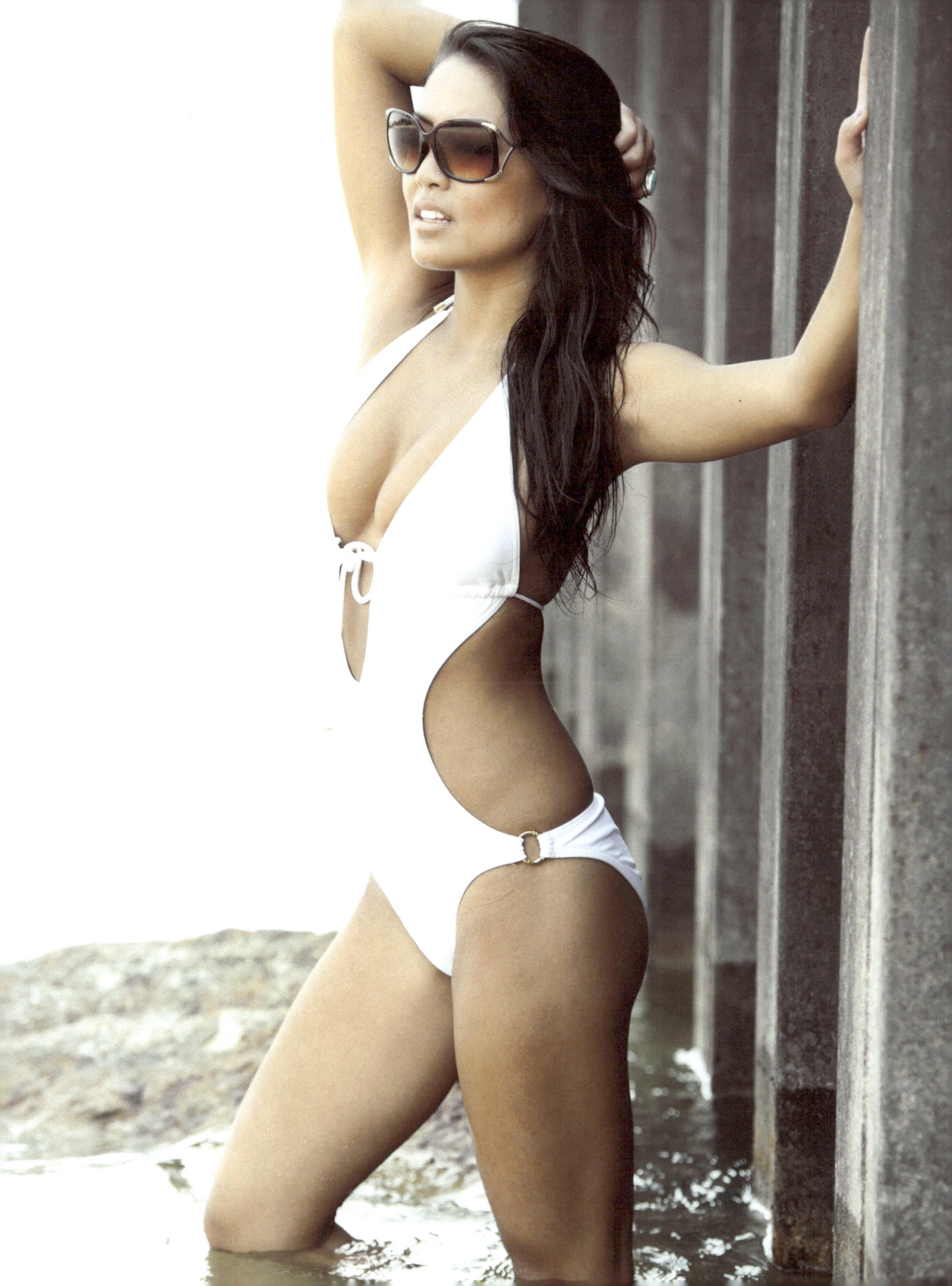

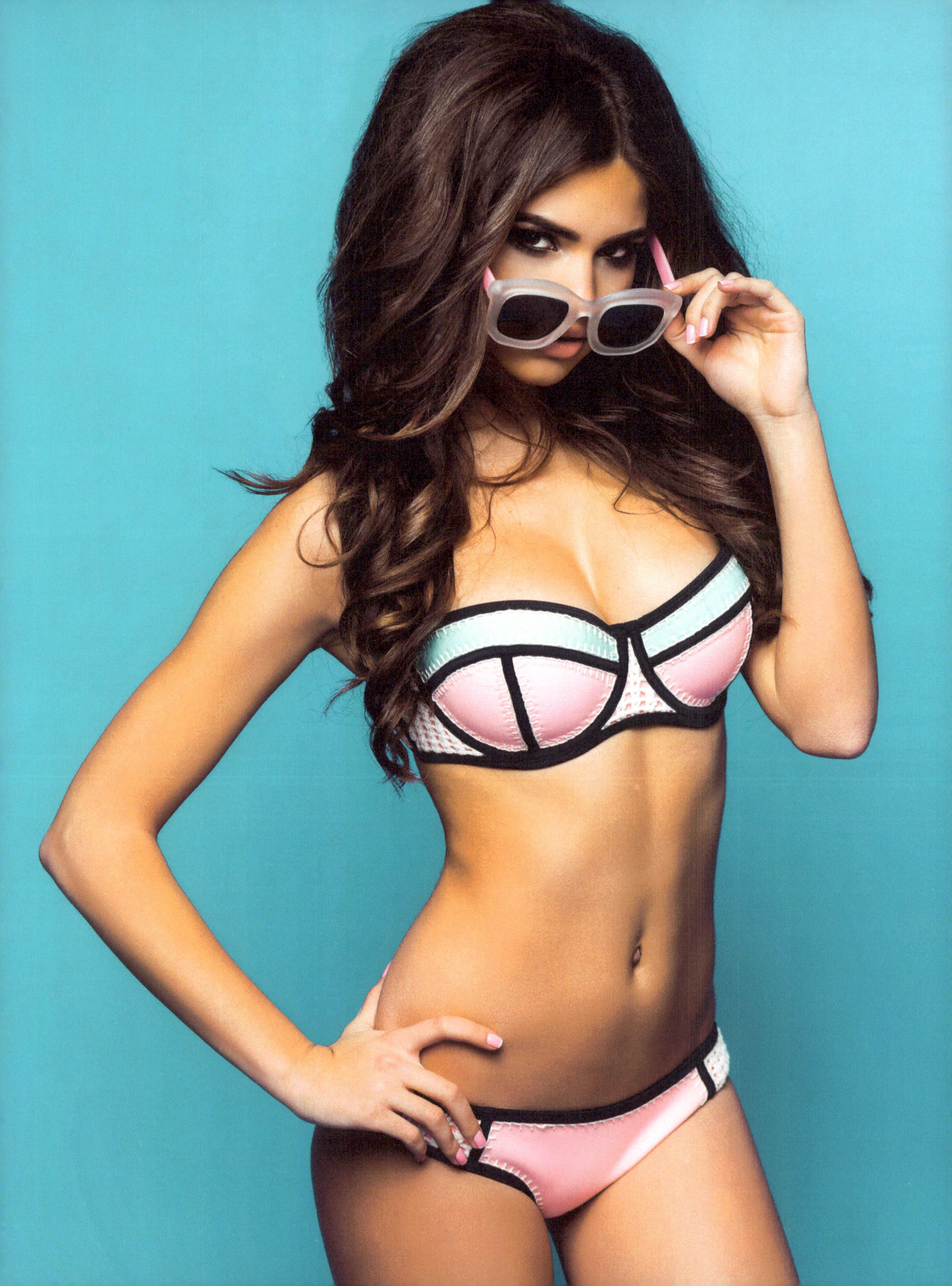

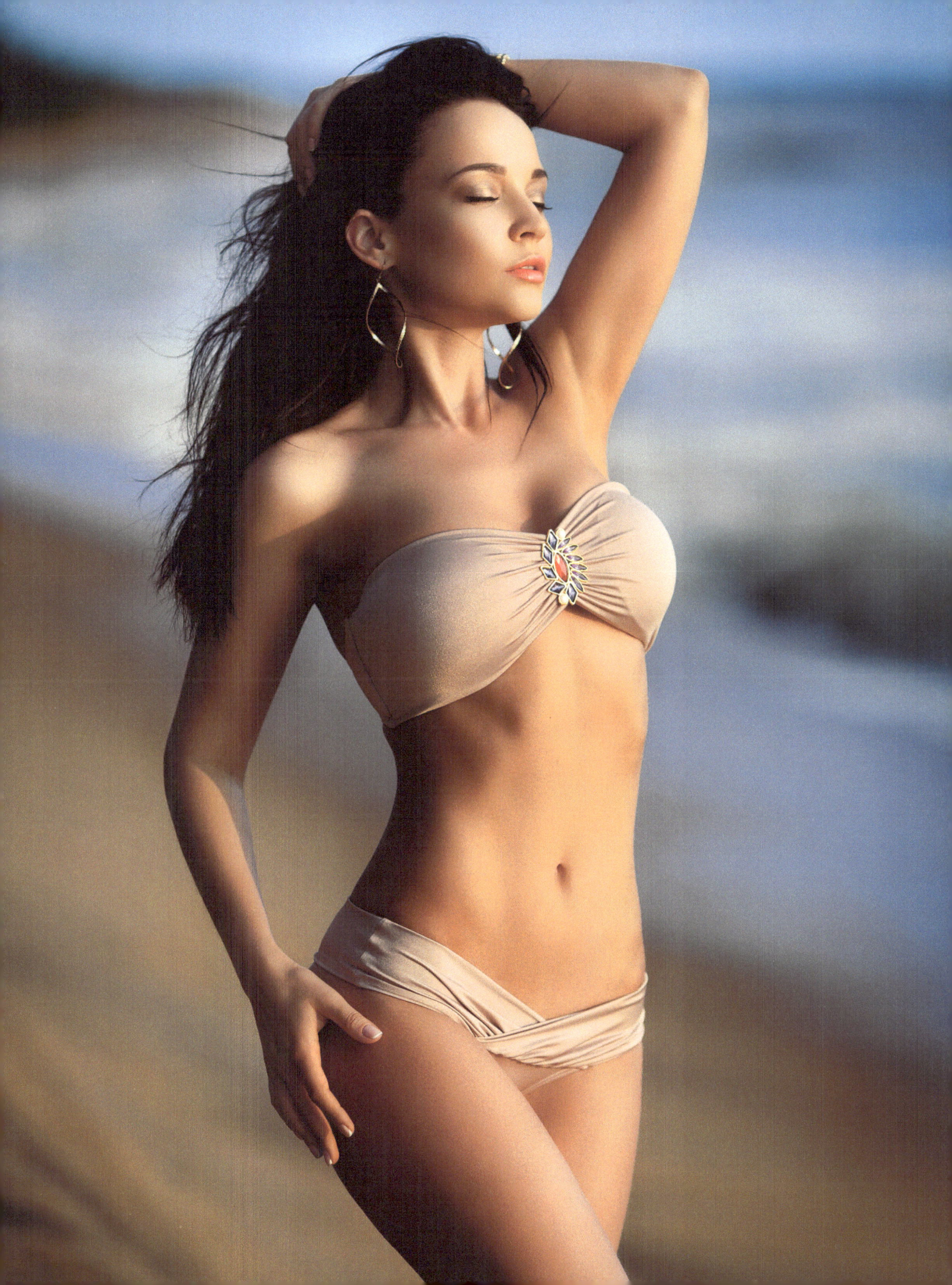

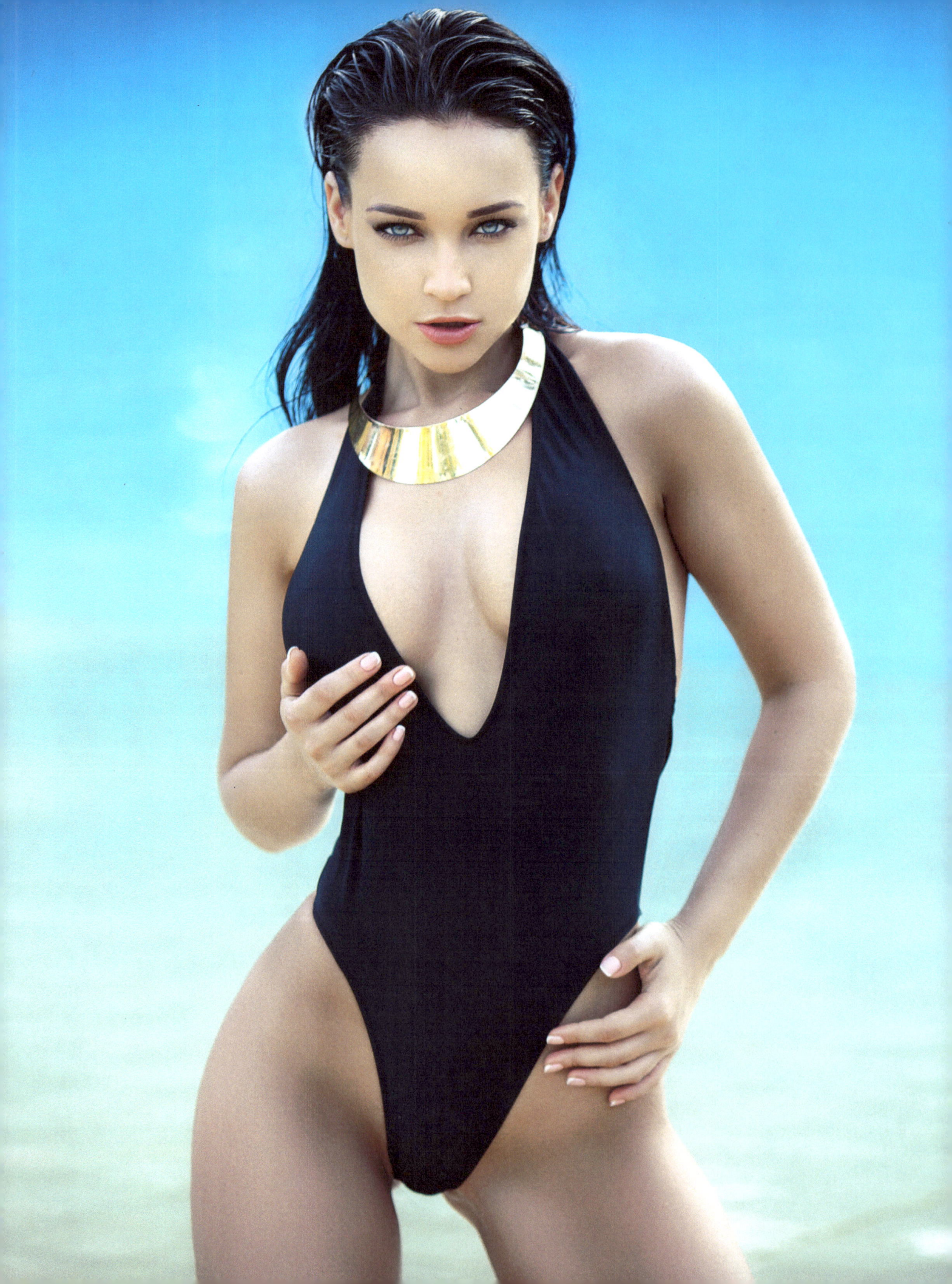

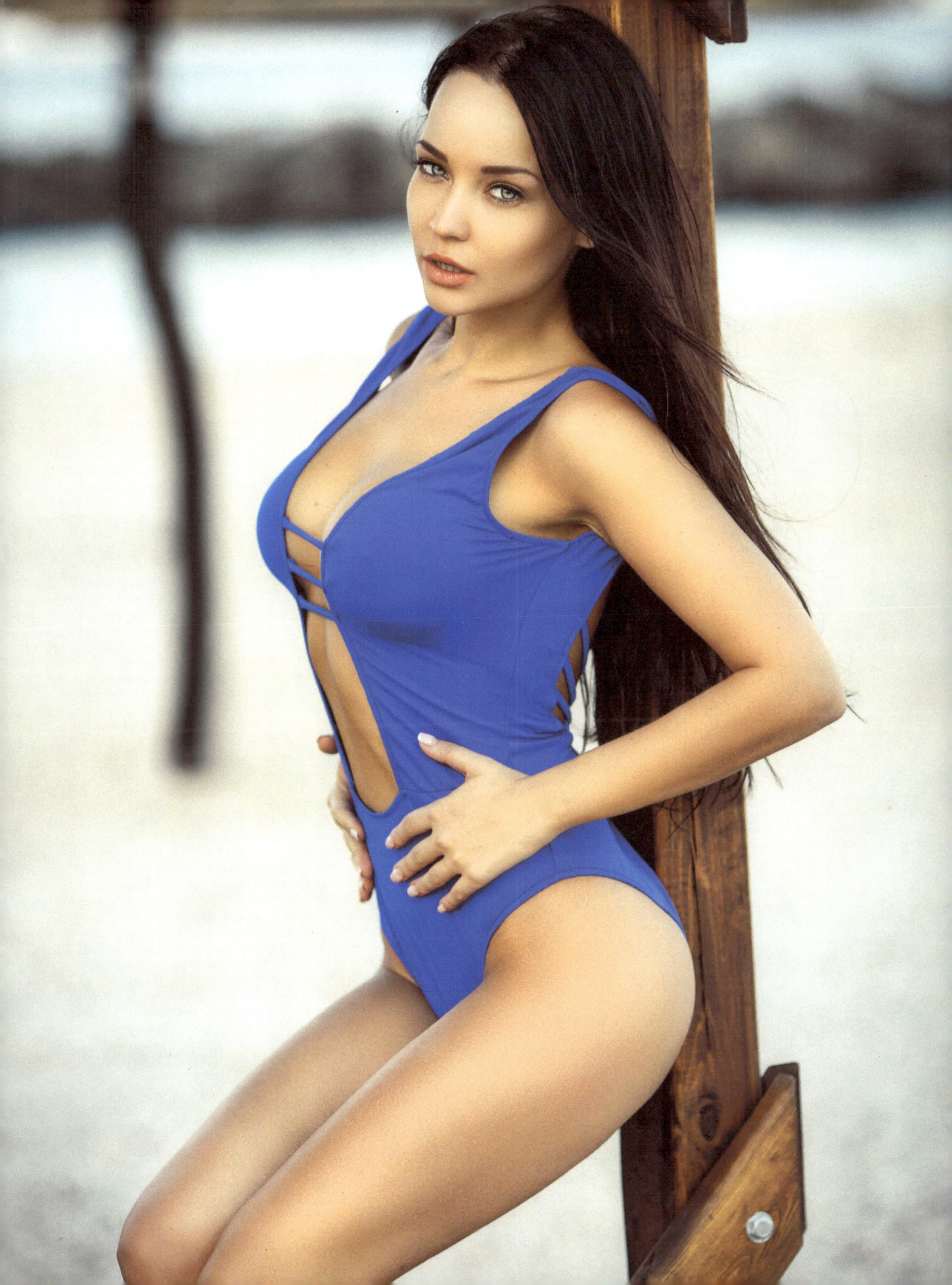

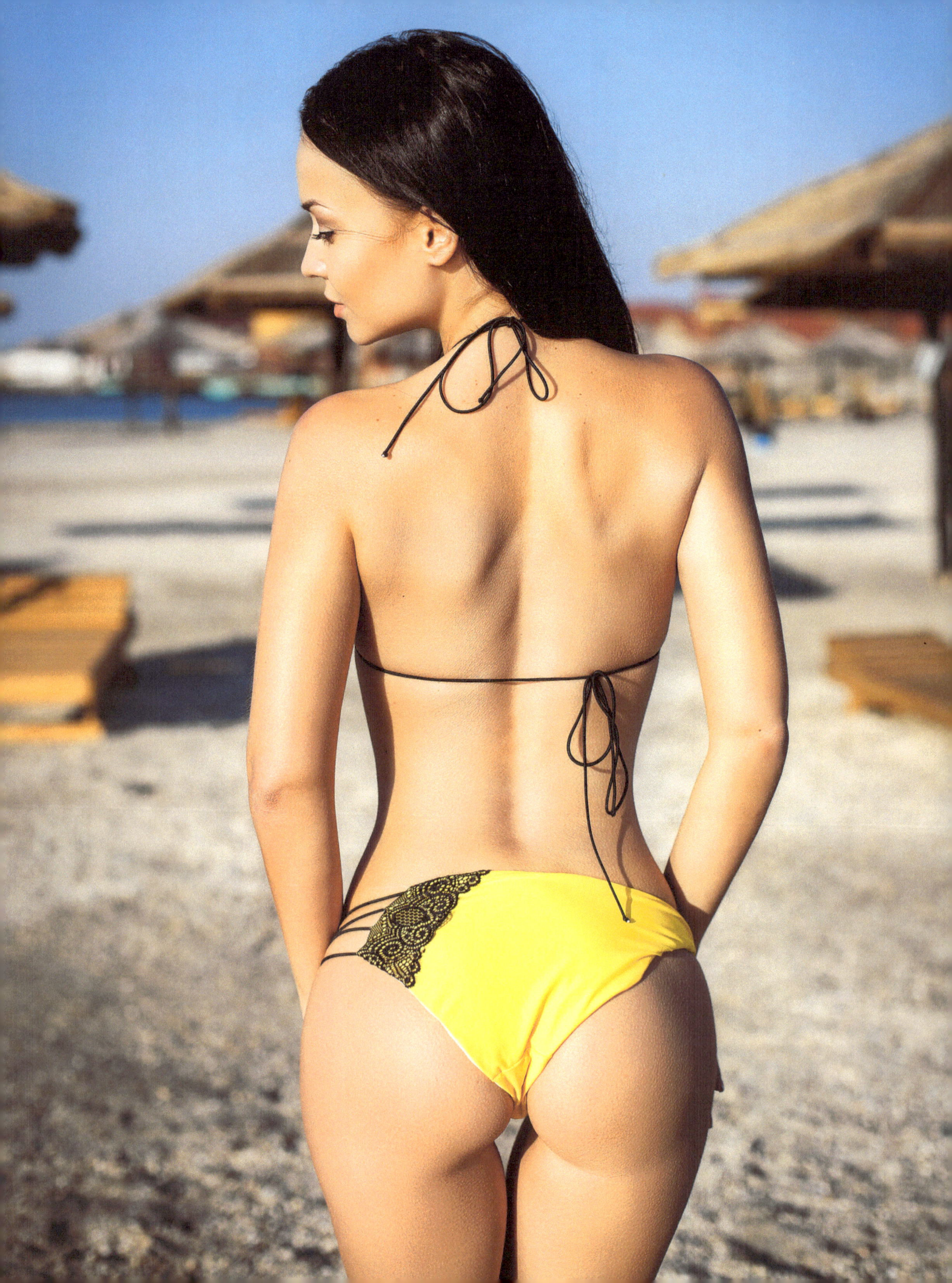

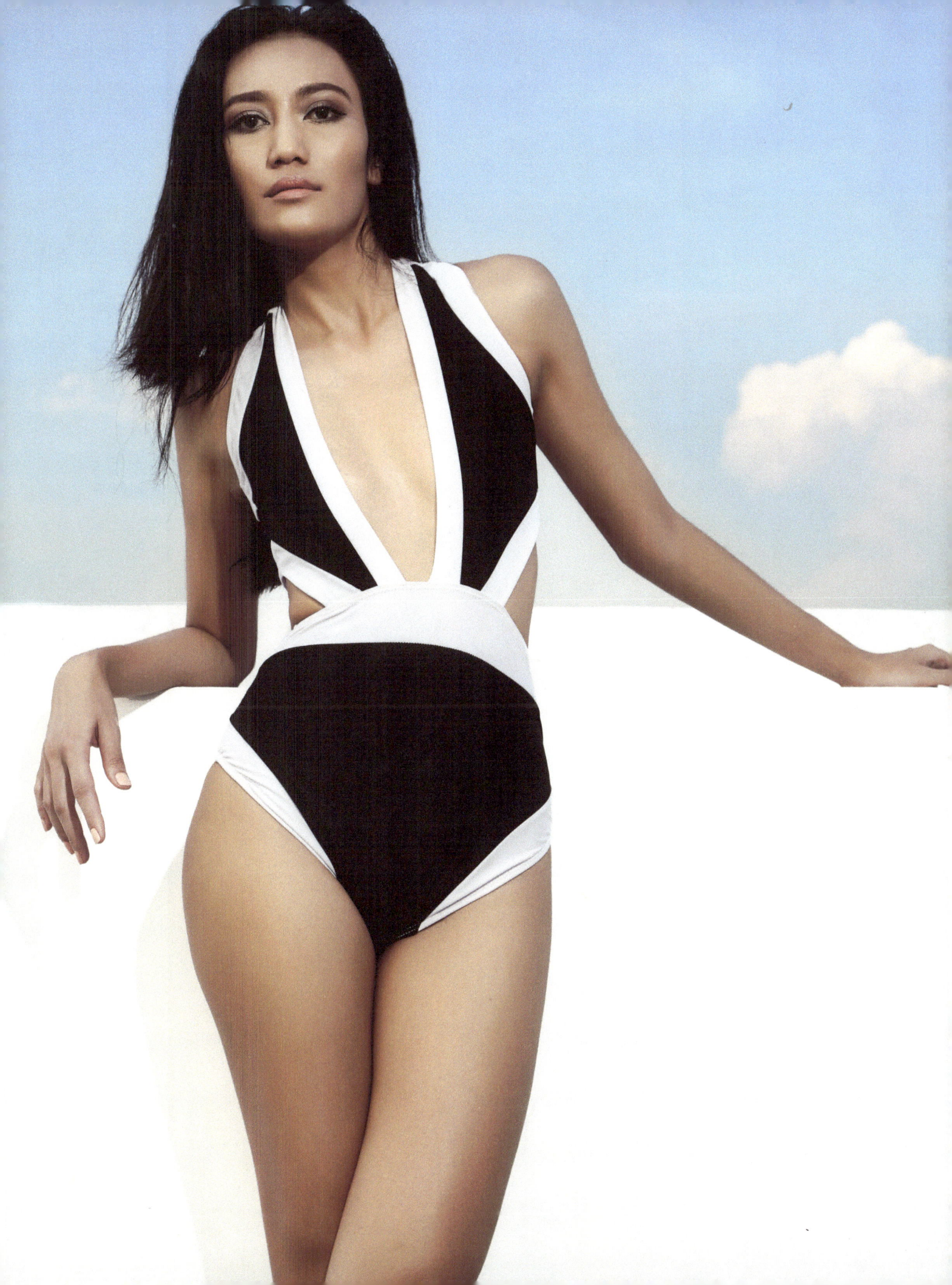

www.ingramcontent.com/pod-product-compliance
Lightning Source LLC
Chambersburg PA
CBHW050417180526
45159CB00005B/2310